ATOMIC

Nature's TRICKS

PAUL MASON

Raintree

www.raintreepublishers.co.uk
Visit our website to find out more information about **Raintree** books.

To order:
 Phone 44 (0) 1865 888112
Send a fax to 44 (0) 1865 314091
Visit the Raintree bookshop at **www.raintreepublishers.co.uk** to browse
our catalogue and order online.

First published in Great Britain by Raintree,
Halley Court, Jordan Hill, Oxford OX2 8EJ, part
of Harcourt Education. Raintree is a registered
trademark of Harcourt Education Ltd.

© Harcourt Education Ltd 2008
First published in paperback in 2008
The moral right of the proprietor has been asserted.

Editorial: Melanie Waldron and Catherine Clarke
Design: Victoria Bevan and Bigtop
Picture Research: Hannah Taylor
Production: Julie Carter

Originated by Chroma Graphics
Printed and bound in China by Leo Paper Group

ISBN 978 1 4062 0680 7 (hardback)
12 11 10 09 08
10 9 8 7 6 5 4 3 2 1

ISBN: 978 1 4062 0701 9 (paperback)
13 12 11 10 09
10 9 8 7 6 5 4 3 2 1

British Library Cataloguing in Publication Data
Mason, Paul
Nature's Tricks. – (Nature's spies) (Atomic)
591
A full catalogue record for this book is available
from the British Library.

Acknowledgements
The publishers would like to thank the following
for permission to reproduce photographs:
ardea.com pp. **5** (bottom) (D. Burgess), **11** (bottom)
(Steve Hopkin), **15** (Auscape/Densey Clyne), **29**
(Francis Gohier); FLPA pp. **6** (Foto Natura/Edo Van
Uchelen), **11** (top) (Nigel Cattlin), **13** (bottom)
(Minden Pictures/Cyril Ruoso/JH Editorial), **22**
(Minden Pictures/Tom Vezo); Naturepl.com pp. **5**
(top) (Phil Savoie), **13** (top) (Anup Shah), **18** (Kim
Taylor), **19** (Kim Taylor), **25** (bottom) (George
McCarthy), **27** (bottom) (Brandon Cole); Oxford
Scientific Films p. **25** (top); Photolibrary pp. **9**
(bottom) (Animals Animals/Earth Scenes), **17**
(Satoshi Kuribayashi), **21** (Konrad Wothe); Seapics.
com pp. **9** (top) (John C. Lewis), **27** (top).

Cover photograph (top) of a Venus flytrap
reproduced with permission of Oxford Scientific
Films (David M. Dennis). Cover photograph (bottom)
of a humpback whale reproduced with permission of
Oxford Scientific Films (Pacific Stock/Watt, Jim).

The publishers would like to thank Nancy Harris,
Diana Bentley, and Dee Reid for their assistance in
the preparation of this book.

Contents

Tricky World 4–5

Types of Trick 6–7

The Artful Anglerfish 8–9

The Killer Flytrap 10–11

Chimp Ant-ics 12–13

Net-throwing Spiders 14–15

Long-jumping Spiders 16–17

Accurate Archer Fish 18–19

The Home Makeover Kings 20–21

The Pretending Plover 22–23

The Crafty Cuckoo 24–25

Bubble-blowing Whales 26–27

The Cleverest Trickster 28–29

Glossary 30

Want to Know More? 31

Index 32

Some words are printed in bold, **like this**. You can find out what they mean in the glossary. You can also look in the box at the bottom of the page where the word first appears.

TRICKY WORLD

What do we mean by "nature's tricks"? We mean the clever techniques some animals and plants use for surviving.

Useful tricks

Why do animals and plants use tricks? Often their goal is to capture food. **Predators** have several tricks for catching their **prey**. Find out about chimps' tricks on pages 12 and 13.

Other animals use tricks for protection – they don't want to become a predator's dinner! One of these is the piping plover – find out more on pages 22 to 23.

Animals also use surprising behaviour to find a mate. Find out about the bowerbird on pages 20 and 21.

predator	animal that hunts other animals for food
prey	animal that is caught and eaten by another animal

This bird of paradise displays its colourful feathers to attract a mate!

These bugs are shaped like thorns to blend in with branches and keep them safe from predators.

This grass snake is pretending to be dead, in the hope that prey will be fooled into coming closer!

TYPES OF TRICK

Some of nature's tricks make the animal world a dangerous place. A seemingly friendly light might actually be leading the way into a **predator's** jaws!

Playing dead

Some animals pretend to be injured or dead. They might be attempting:

✷ To protect their young by drawing predators away from their nest.

✷ To attract **prey**. Once the prey is in range, they leap into action. Too late, it becomes obvious they are not really injured at all!

Learning new tricks

The cleverest animals are able to acquire new tricks. They can alter the way they hunt, depending on what has succeeded for them in the past.

That's amazing!

"Pitcher plants" have a rolled-up leaf with sweet-smelling water inside. But the sides are slippery – any insects that crawl in cannot climb out!

THE ARTFUL ANGLERFISH

Imagine a small predator fish swimming in the deep, dark ocean. It sees a light in the distance and investigates, believing there might be prey ahead.

The small predator swims up to the light, but suddenly everything goes dark. It has been swallowed whole! The light wasn't something to eat – it was a larger predator! It was a clever, hungry anglerfish.

Did you know?

Some anglerfish can "walk" along the seabed using their fins.

ANGLERFISH

HABITAT: oceans so deep that sunlight does not reach the bottom

Special spine dangles in front of the anglerfish's mouth

Tip of spine glows in the dark and attracts other fish

The anglerfish can make its mouth and stomach stretch to a size that allows it to swallow its prey whole!

THE KILLER FLYTRAP

We expect animals to eat plants, but some plants have turned the tables, and cunningly trick animals into being eaten!

Hungry plants

The most famous **carnivorous** plant is the Venus flytrap.

No escape

When it catches an insect, the flytrap's leaves close so tightly that no air can enter. The plant releases liquids that dissolve the insect's body into food. Soon all that remains is the shell. The trap opens, and the shell blows away.

VENUS FLYTRAP

HABITAT:
coastal North and South Carolina, USA

carnivorous   **meat-eating**

nectar   **sweet liquid that plants use to attract insects**

The Venus flytrap's leaves let out a sweet-smelling **nectar** that attracts insects. When the insects touch the "trigger" hairs – SNAP – the leaves shut tight!

"Trigger" hairs

Struggle as it might, this fly is unlikely to escape from the flytrap's clutches.

CHIMP ANT-ICS

Not all animals wait for their victims to come to them. The chimpanzee actively searches for **prey** to trick.

Snack attack!

Chimps like to eat ants and **termites**, but their plump chimp fingers cannot squeeze into the little holes where ants and termites dwell. The clever chimps have discovered a way to fish for their prey.

A chimp finds a twig and pulls off the leaves. It sticks the twig inside the hole and waits for the insects to crawl on to it. The chimp pulls the twig out, and the ants or termites quickly become a chimp snack!

CHIMPANZEE HABITAT: **equatorial** and rainforest areas in Africa

equatorial	from a region near the equator, an imaginary line that runs around the middle of Earth
termite	small, ant-like animal

This chimp is hoping to catch itself a string of termites.

This clever chimp is using a leaf as a drinking cup.

NET-THROWING SPIDERS

Most people think of spiders as animals that catch prey in webs, but not all spiders wait for their meal to arrive.

Spinning a net

Net-throwing spiders have a special trick for catching their prey. As the Sun sets, they spin a net, not a web. Then they go hunting...

First the spider uses its front four arms to hold the net. Next, it hangs upside down somewhere it might catch some dinner. If anything passes by, the spider throws its net, then pulls it up and eats its victim!

NET-THROWING SPIDERS

HABITAT: warmer parts of the Americas, Africa, and Australia

This female is just starting to spin her net.

LONG-JUMPING SPIDERS

Some spiders do not bother with a web, or even a net. They have come up with an alternative trick for catching their prey!

Jumping spiders

Jumping spiders leap out of a hiding place to catch their prey. They can leap huge distances – up to 50 times their own length. If humans could do that, they would be able to jump almost 100 metres (328 feet)!

That's amazing!

How do jumping spiders jump so far? A muscle in its body squeezes liquid into the spider's legs, causing them to expand. The spider then leaps forwards, as if it had powerful pogo sticks attached to its legs!

This jumping spider leaps through the air towards its victim.

ARCHER FISH

HABITAT:
India and
Southeast Asia

Large eyes – good
for spotting insects

Dark and light pattern –
even harder to see because
they look like ripples or
shadows under the surface

Narrow body – hard
to see from above

Ready...aim...fire! The
archer fish bags a meal!

unique   one of a kind

ACCURATE ARCHER FISH

Insects provide plenty of food for fish. One fish has a **unique trick** for catching insects.

Fishy sharpshooters

The archer fish hunts insects by shooting them with water! The fish makes a tube with its tongue, sticks the tip of its mouth above the surface, and takes aim. Out squirts a jet of water, and this knocks the insect out of the air! The moment the insect lands on the surface, the fish gobbles it down.

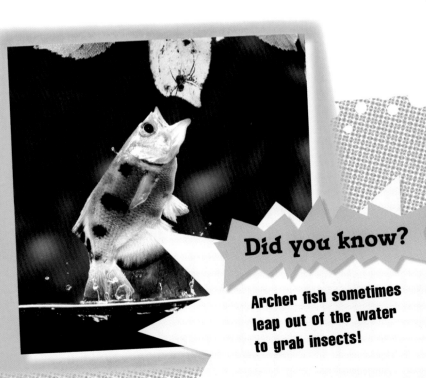

Did you know?

Archer fish sometimes leap out of the water to grab insects!

THE HOME MAKEOVER KINGS

Not all animals employ special tricks for hunting – some use their skills to attract a mate.

Looking for love

Male bowerbirds build their **bower** to attract a female. They decorate their bower with brightly coloured objects. These can include flowers, leaves, and bits of plastic, glass, or paper.

The bowerbird is very particular about where everything is placed. If he leaves and one of the bright objects is stirred, he gets distraught. Immediately he puts the object back in its original place!

Did you know?

Sometimes, cheeky bowerbirds steal bright things from their neighbour's bower!

bower shady, leafy shelter usually found in woodland areas

BOWERBIRD

HABITAT:
Australia and
New Guinea

Bowerbirds themselves are not usually very colourful, but they like to have bright homes!

PIPING PLOVER

HABITAT:
northwest
Atlantic beaches

This piping plover has not really hurt its wing – it is trying to lure a predator away from its nest.

THE PRETENDING PLOVER

Some animals use tricks to defend their young when a **predator** approaches. They pretend to be injured. The predator believes it has found an easy meal, and follows them away from their young.

Nesting on the ground

The piping plover builds its nest on the ground where predators such as rats could eat its chicks. Luckily, the chicks are very well **camouflaged** and hard to spot!

When predators approach

When predators come close, the plover moves away. It drags its wing along the ground as if it is broken, tricking the predator into following it. Once the predator is lured far away from the chicks, the plover flies off.

camouflage — **way of hiding by blending in with your surroundings, or disguising yourself**

THE CRAFTY CUCKOO

Most animals spend a great deal of time looking after their young, but one bird has developed a trick so that it doesn't have to look after its chicks!

Guest in the nest

Cuckoos lay their egg in the nest of another bird, while the owners are away. The owners do not realize that this is a new egg. The cuckoo's egg and the owner's eggs have similar markings.

Once the baby cuckoo hatches, it shoves all the other eggs or baby birds from the nest. This ensures it will not have to share the food!

Did you know?

Baby cuckoos can imitate the calls of non-cuckoo chicks.

imitate   copy

The large egg does not belong in this nest – it's a cuckoo egg.

This cuckoo chick has hatched in a reed warbler's nest.

BUBBLE-BLOWING WHALES

Humpback whales feed by taking in huge mouthfuls of seawater. The water escapes from the whale's mouth, and the fish are swallowed whole!

Catching lots of fish – a guide for young whales

This trick helps humpback whales make sure every mouthful has plenty of fish:

1. In deep water, the whale swims around in a circle. It blows out a long stream of air bubbles. The circle of air bubbles rises towards the surface and traps fish inside.

2. The fish are driven towards the surface. The whale comes up in the middle of the air circle with its huge mouth wide open. Almost all the fish are swallowed in one giant gulp!

THE CLEVEREST TRICKSTER

Which animal is the best trickster of all? It is probably the killer whale. Killer whales are very intelligent and work out new hunting tricks very quickly.

Trapping seagulls

One gang of killer whales in Canada tricks seagulls. They spit bits of dead fish on to the surface of the sea. When a seagull comes for the fish scraps, the whale grabs it and swallows it whole!

Hunting seals

Other killer whales work in teams to catch seals. Two or three whales swim where they can be spotted by the seals. Meanwhile, another whale swims silently towards the beach.

Suddenly, the sneaky whale swims up on to the beach. It grabs a seal, and then wriggles back into the sea.

| intelligent | clever, and able to learn new skills quickly |

This seal felt safe on the beach just moments ago. Now it's a killer whale's lunch!

Glossary

bower shady, leafy shelter usually found in woodland areas

camouflage way of hiding by blending in with your surroundings, or disguising yourself

carnivorous meat-eating. Lions, tigers, wolves, sharks, and even some plants are carnivorous.

equatorial from a region near the equator, an imaginary line that runs around the middle of Earth

imitate copy. Being able to imitate the noises another animal makes means sounding just like them.

intelligent clever, and able to learn new skills quickly

nectar sweet liquid that plants use to attract insects. As the insects move from plant to plant, they help the plants to reproduce (make new versions of themselves).

predator animal that hunts other animals for food

prey animal that is caught and eaten by another animal

termite small, ant-like animal

unique one of a kind

Want to Know More?

Books

* *Animals Head to Head: Shark vs. Killer Whale*, Isabel Thomas (Raintree, 2006)

* *Life in the Undergrowth*, David Attenborough (BBC Books, 2005)

* *Wild Predators: Deadly Spiders and Scorpions*, Andrew Solway (Heinemann Library, 2005)

Websites

* http://science.howstuffworks.com
  Type "spiders" or "Venus flytrap" into the search field to find out more about how they work!

* www.yahooligans.com
  Type "chimpanzee" or "piping plover" into this search engine and follow the links to find out more about these amazing animals.

If you liked this Atomic book, why don't you try these...?

Index

anglerfish 8–9
archer fish 18–19

birds 5, 20–25
birds of paradise 5
bowerbirds 20–21
bugs 5

camouflage 5, 23
carnivorous plants 7, 10–11
chicks, protecting 23, 25
chimpanzees 12–13
cuckoos 24–25

drinking cups 13

fish 8–9, 18–19
food 4, 8, 10, 12, 14, 19, 26, 28

grass snakes 6

humpback whales 26–27
hunting tricks 6–19, 12–13, 26, 28

injured or dead, pretending to be 6, 7, 22, 23
intelligence 28

jumping spiders 16–17

killer whales 28–29

mate, attracting a 4, 5, 20–21

nectar 10, 11
net-throwing spiders 14–15
new tricks, learning 7, 28

piping plovers 22–23
pitcher plants 7
plants 7, 10–11
predators 4, 5, 7, 8, 23
prey 4, 7, 8, 12, 16
protection tricks 4, 7, 22–23

seals 28, 29
spiders 14–17

termites 12, 13
trigger hairs 11

Venus flytrap 10–11

whales 26–29

Notes for adults
Use the following questions to guide children towards identifying features of report text:
Can you find an example of a general opening classification on page 4?
Can you give an example of a generic participant on page 10?
Can you find the details of how a whale catches fish on page 26?
Can you give examples of present tense language on page 28?